Oxford Scene

First published in Great Britain in 1994 by
Chris Andrews Publications
15 Curtis Yard
North Hinksey Lane
Oxford OX2 0LX
Tel: + 44 (0)1865-723404
Web: www.cap-ox.com
Reprinted 1994
Updated and reprinted 1997, 2000, 2004, 2006.

Photographed and produced by Chris Andrews,
all pictures from
The Oxford Picture Library.
Text by David Huelin
Design by Mike Brain
Printed and bound in Great Britain by Butler and Tanner Ltd

ISBN 10: 0 9509643 4 4
ISBN 13: 978 0 9509643 4 8

Front cover – *Central Oxford from Trinity College Tower*
Back cover – *Oxford from South Parks*
Title page – *The City from the North*

Oxford Scene

Photographed by Chris Andrews

Contents

INTRODUCTION

The Vice-Chancellor of Oxford University (1993–1997), Sir Peter North, C.B.E., Q.C., D.C.L., F.B.A.

Eight hundred years of intellectual endeavour have given Oxford University its worldwide reputation as a place to which scholars come to study, teach and do research in a wide variety of disciplines. Pride in the achievements of the University has led over the centuries to benefactions of many kinds, some of great munificence, which have had a striking impact on Oxford's architecture. Unlike so many other European university cities, Oxford has been fortunate to be spared the ravages of war, avoiding both damage in the English Civil War and aerial bombardment in the Second World War, and the result is a city of architectural delight.

The Oxford of today comprises not only fine University buildings, both ancient and very modern, but also college buildings with their quadrangles and gardens, exemplifying the variety of the thirty-nine different colleges. This architectural heritage was created as a consequence of groups of students gathering together at the feet of renowned scholars, and this practice in effect continues today, with the result that the colleges are neither museums nor mere halls of residence, but living communities of scholars, young and old. Not only do new generations of students year by year enjoy this heritage of University and colleges combined; so also do thousands of visitors, and so may you through the pages of this book, with its splendid and evocative photographs. Handsome buildings, exquisite detail and engaging vistas – all are portrayed here – and all make up the beauty that is Oxford.

The Radcliffe Camera, St Mary's Church and Merton College Chapel.

OXFORD

Oxford has been the home of England's oldest university since before the year 1200. There were then three monastic schools with some tradition of learning, and when in 1167 the English scholars at the University of Paris were obliged to leave, King Henry II persuaded many of them to come to Oxford. They brought their experience of the ancient curriculum of studies in force at Paris and they set up a similar course in Oxford.

The system was based on a guild of Masters to which scholars, after seven years' studies in the liberal arts, would be admitted with a licence to teach, and some obligation to do so. All teaching was under the Church (of Rome) and all scholars, Masters, and Doctors were in holy orders, tonsured, and wearing a long black gown.

The scholars were of humble parentage; in an age when the nobility were illiterate and there were no middle classes, the administration of Church and State depended on educated clerks in holy orders. The monastery schools offered intelligent boys a way into the University as scholars; a degree would enable them to become teachers or to aspire to comfortable church livings or well-rewarded offices of State.

At Oxford the Masters' guild, known as *universitas*, was well established by the year 1200; it was confirmed by the Church in 1214 with the appointment of a Chancellor. Once the University was recognized, Oxford attracted an influx of scholars, many of them very young, who engendered some disorder and friction with the townspeople; this broke out from time to time in violent "town-and-gown" riots. The University owned no buildings before 1320 and was free to move; some of the riots caused migrations of Masters and scholars to other towns, including Cambridge where in 1209 they founded or enlarged the nucleus of another university.

The Masters began in the 13th century to gather the young scholars into halls of residence where they might have adequate living quarters and protection from a hostile town, and would be subject to some discipline. Eventually a certain amount of teaching was done in the halls and some of them gained a good reputation, but they were impermanent since each depended on the enterprise of a Master who in turn had to obtain the approval of the guild. Academic halls came and went; the names of some two hundred have been recorded, though

University College.

probably not more than eighty existed at any one time in the 13th and 14th centuries.

By the beginning of the 15th century the halls had academic status, and in 1420 a Royal Statute decreed that students would be admitted to the University only when they were matriculated (enrolled) at a recognised Academic Hall or College.

The first endowed colleges appeared at the same time as the halls, in the 13th century, but their origins and aims were different. The secular priests who had become rich churchmen and ministers of the Crown were under Church rules celibate, and had no openly recognised progeny to inherit their wealth. A commendable act was to found and endow a college, primarily for "Founder's Kin", to prepare priests for rewarding places in Church and State, and for scholars to pray for the Founder's soul.

The first colleges in Oxford – up to the Reformation – were not in competition with the halls, but they were a secular reply to the monasteries, with their secure buildings, good living, and internal discipline; besides this the colleges could encourage more adventurous thinking than was normal in a monastery. That was important, and the founders of two colleges expressly forbade their members to make any monastic vow.

Though not in calculated competition with the halls, the colleges' financial resources, ownership of their buildings, and above all their permanence, with statutes and elected Fellows, meant that they were able to do more effectively everything that the halls did, especially from the 15th century when scholars as well as Masters were lodged and boarded all under one roof. The medieval halls slowly disappeared; with one exception they were either closed or bought and absorbed by their rich college neighbours.

The first three colleges were founded within a few years of each other in the 13th century: University College ("Univ"), Merton, and

Balliol. The question of which is the oldest rests on the definition of foundation: the endowment; the ownership of permanent buildings; or the royal approval of statutes. However, St Edmund Hall, the sole survivor of the medieval halls, can claim to be the oldest teaching establishment, already in existence half a century before the first three colleges.

Four colleges were set up in the 14th century: Exeter, Oriel, Queen's, and New College. The founder of this last, William of Wykeham, set a pattern for college life when he stipulated that scholars should live in college and be taught by resident Masters, who would cover the whole university curriculum in the Faculty of Arts – that is, for a Master's degree. The practice of scholars living in college and "reading with a Master" became general.

In the 15th century three colleges were founded by rich prelates: Lincoln, All Souls, and Magdalen. They were set up on medieval lines, the members being enjoined to pray for the Founder's soul and to prepare themselves to defend the Faith and combat heresy. Two more colleges were founded early in the 16th century before the Reformation: Brasenose and Corpus Christi.

The 16th century is remarkable for the founding of Christ Church by King Henry VIII in 1546, despite the upheaval of the Reformation. He completed part of the great college conceived by Cardinal Wolsey, and thereby gave his approval to the University, which some "greedy souls" would have dissolved for its revenues.

The Dissolution of the Monasteries had the effect of cutting off Oxford's supply of young monastic scholars; however, from the Elizabethan age the rising middle classes increasingly demanded a university education for their sons, and were willing to pay for it; the colleges were glad to accept the fees, and the "gentleman commoner", who was not a member of the foundation but more like a paying guest, crowded out the tonsured indigent scholar.

Christ Church, Tom Tower.

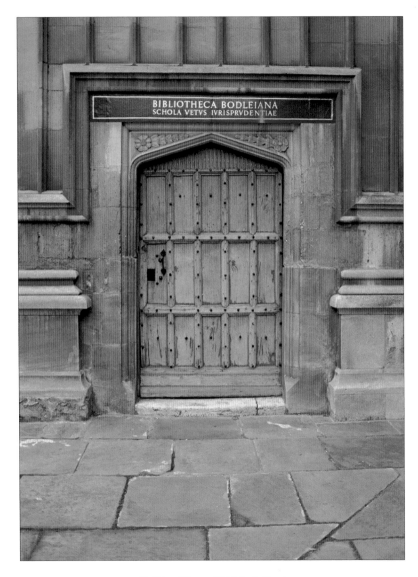

Bodleian Library, Old Schools Quad.

After the Reformation and the founding of Christ Church three colleges were set up in the 16th century: Trinity, St John's, and Jesus, bringing the total to thirteen.

The rather rapid expansion of the colleges, each with its group of buildings, was not accompanied by a parallel material growth of the University. From its beginnings in the 12th century for more than a hundred years the Masters' guild owned no building; important ceremonials, ecclesiastical trials, and even the day-to-day business of the Masters – including making loans to scholars from the University Chest – all were conducted in the nave of St Mary the Virgin, known as the University Church. The modest Congregation House built in 1320 adjoining the north-east corner of the church provided a sort of committee room for the Masters, with an upper floor for the incipient library, but for major events they still used the church, and the University had no visible material presence.

Similarly the teaching side had no lecture-halls of its own until a century later, when about 1420 the Masters began to build proper lecture-rooms to replace the inadequate medieval hovels that were still being used. These early "schools" (faculty) buildings, standing where the Old Schools Quadrangle is today, were the first visible expression of the University in a town that already had several impressive college buildings.

The 16th century saw no university building until 1598 when Sir Thomas Bodley began the restoration of Duke Humfrey's Library – part of the 1420 buildings – and eventually the rebuilding of the schools quadrangle with three floors, the topmost storey being reserved for the rapidly growing library.

The expansive character of the Elizabethan age saw a great increase in academic activity and a rapid broadening of the fields of learning. This continued under James I; the University basked in his patronage, and Jacobean architecture sprang up all over Oxford.

Two colleges were founded: Wadham and Pembroke; and in 1624 Sir Thomas Bodley's great library scheme was completed.

With Charles I on the throne, William Laud – successively Fellow and President of St John's, Chancellor of the University, confidant of the King, and Archbishop of Canterbury – drafted a new Statute for the University, known as the Caroline or Laudian Code of 1636; it created some resentment but it effectively regulated the University for many years.

During the Civil War the occupation of Oxford by the King, his Court, his army, and all the hangers-on, brought academic activity virtually to a standstill; many of the Fellows and most of the students disappeared. The colleges, in their royalist fervour, contributed loans to the King's exchequer – never repaid – and handed over much of their enormously valuable silver to be melted down for coinage.

The rule of the Commonwealth, though bitterly resented by staunch Royalists, brought about a revival of academic activity. Oliver Cromwell was Chancellor in 1650–57; as a Cambridge graduate he took Oxford's needs seriously, and the Parliamentarian appointments to vacated fellowships were acknowledged, even by Royalists, to be good scholars.

The Restoration revived Oxford's confidence, and Archbishop Gilbert Sheldon, a former Warden of All Souls and later Chancellor, commissioned another All Souls man, Christopher Wren, to design an assembly hall for the ceremonials and sometimes rowdy celebrations that were still being most unsuitably held at St Mary's Church. The Sheldonian Theatre, opened in 1669 was the University's second major building, and it has lost none of its importance over the years.

The 17th century also saw great building activity among the colleges and the emergence of two talented amateur architects: Henry Aldrich, Dean of Christ Church, and George Clarke, Fellow

Academics.

of All Souls, who both, with advice from the professionals such as Wren and Hawksmoor, greatly enriched Oxford architecturally.

The University maintained its sense of importance during the 18th century and was able to add majestically to its material presence with the Clarendon Building and the Radcliffe Camera. The trustees of Dr John Radcliffe's estate also gave Oxford the Radcliffe Infirmary (1770) and the Radcliffe Observatory (1794) with its beautiful Tower of Winds.

These additions to the University's material presence may have stimulated the science faculties but they did little for the Arts, where academic standards were low. The prevailing indolence also affected religious observance, and this deeply offended John and Charles Wesley, both graduates of Christ Church, who in 1729 with some equally indignant friends formed the Holy Club to encourage the primitive spirit of Christianity, and they some years later laid the foundations of the Methodist Church.

Only two colleges were founded in the 18th century – more correctly, refounded, since both had ancient antecedents and some buildings – namely Worcester and Hertford. Building work also went on at All Souls, Queen's, Magdalen, and the Radcliffe Camera.

The 19th century brought in radical reforms and far-reaching changes in university life. When college Fellows were no longer obliged to be in holy orders, were free to marry, and were required to undertake serious teaching or research, men of a different calibre were attracted to university work; the colleges began to elect Fellows for their intellectual capacity rather than for their capacity for port wine, and there were soon erudite men in the colleges.

By the 1870s university life was respectable and interesting and the teaching was serious. The scene was set for the greatest revolution in the University's history: the admission of women. Between 1878 and 1898 four colleges for women and the Society of Home Students

(later St Anne's) were founded; resistance to the advent of women delayed until 1920 their right to receive degrees, and the women's halls – as they technically were – did not acquire full college status until 1959.

The 19th century was remarkably expansive; besides the women's colleges, several major university buildings were put up, including the new Examination Schools in the High Street, the University Press building in Walton Street, the Ashmolean Museum in Beaumont Street, and the University Museum in Parks Road. Virtually all the existing colleges were enlarged, and Keble College was founded and built.

Fourteen new colleges have been established in the 20th century; seven of these already existed in another form and have now achieved independent college status. The logical, even inevitable, outcome of the 19th-century decision to admit women to the University has been the 20th-century admission of women to the men's colleges, and then of men to the women's.

An increasingly perplexing question in this century has been that of university funding; small and irregular amounts of state aid, first made in the 1920s, were replaced in 1945 by systematic funding through the University Grants Committee, an advisory body. In 1981 the Government imposed cuts in university funding; in 1988 the Committee was replaced by the University Funding Council, with greater powers of intervention and financial control; a more stringent attitude has prevailed into the 1990s.

This has caused no little anxiety, especially in the Arts Faculties, whose activities are sometimes of less commercial value. There has been more rapid expansion in the Science Faculties, with industrial companies sponsoring research in the development of commercially useful laboratory discoveries.

Oxford from the west.

Trinity College Chapel from Balliol College gardens.

Christ Church: The House and the Cathedral.

ALL SOULS COLLEGE

Wren's Sundial.

The ninth college foundation; Archbishop Henry Chichele, with King Henry VI, set up the College of All Souls of the Faithful Departed in 1438 as a chantry where prayers would be said for the souls of the King, the Archbishop, and all those who had died in the wars against France. Chichele's second aim was the forming of competent administrators of Church and State. The foundation provided for a Warden and forty Fellows, who should be graduates or mature scholars studying for doctorates.

All Souls has never altered its statutes so as to admit undergraduates, but it welcomes as Fellows distinguished academics from other universities as well as Oxford; the membership is now nearer seventy. Christopher Wren was a Fellow, and Bursar, of the College; he designed the sundial now on the south wall of the Codrington Library. The buildings belong to two distinct periods; the front quadrangle on the High Street, including the chapel, but not the hall, is largely original 15th-century.

The twin towers, with the hall and the Codrington Library in the North Quad, are the work of Dr George Clarke, Warden of the College, and Nicholas Hawksmoor, dating from 1714–34.

The Chapel.

The College from the east and central Oxford over Queen's College.

THE ASHMOLEAN MUSEUM
AND THE TAYLOR INSTITUTION

The Museum front.

This classical neo-Grecian building of 1845, by the talented Charles R. Cockerell, is the outcome of three coinciding bequests: two towards housing the University's growing collection of art treasures, and one for improving language studies. This accounts for the presence in one building of such dissimilar occupants as the University Galleries and the Taylor Institution. Elias Ashmole's collection was redistributed in the 1850s, and the paintings and sculptures came to the newly built University Galleries; in the following years the Galleries were greatly enriched by gifts and bequests, and in 1899 were renamed the Ashmolean Museum. Today it ranks as one of the most important art galleries in Britain. The "Taylorian" is the centre of studies in modern European (principally Western) languages, and it possesses a magnificent multilingual library. It occupies the east wing of the building, facing onto St Giles; the four huge Ionic columns are surmounted by statues representing France, Italy, Germany and Spain.

The Taylor Institution showing the four Ionic columns.

BALLIOL COLLEGE

Broad Street Front.

Balliol is one of the three oldest college foundations and was the first to occupy a site of its own, which it still stands on. John de Balliol, of Barnard Castle, in 1260 quarrelled with the Bishop of Durham but lost the argument; part of his penance was to set up in Oxford a house for sixteen poor scholars and to support them. By 1263 he had established a tenement of some kind, but he died in 1269 without having made adequate endowments; his widow Princess Dervorguilla completed the task.

The college remained rather obscure until about 1800; then a succession of four Masters – John Parsons, Richard Jenkyns, Robert Scott, Benjamin Jowett – who spanned the 19th century, achieved Balliol's reputation for academic excellence. Although the college stands on its original 13th century site, there is only one ancient building: the old library of about 1480. The rest of the college is chiefly 19th-century, beginning with the "Balmoral Gothic" of the Broad Street front.

Front Quad and Gate-tower.

Garden Quad and Chapel.

The Fellows' Garden with "Dervorguilla's Tomb".

THE BODLEIAN LIBRARY

The University's first library was set up in the 14th century in the Old Congregation House adjoining St Mary's Church, the first building owned by the University. About a century later Humfrey Duke of Gloucester, a Balliol man, younger brother of Henry V, began giving books and manuscripts to the library, and the enlarged collection was housed on the upper floor of the Divinity School, completed in 1489, and named Duke Humfrey's Library.

These books were later destroyed or dispersed by the Puritan Visitation of 1549, and the building remained empty and neglected or used as a pig market for half a century. But in 1598 Sir Thomas Bodley, formerly of Merton, retired from the Queen's diplomatic service and set about restoring and re-stocking the library. So many books accrued that by 1612 Bodley had added the east wing (the "Arts End") to Duke Humfrey's Library and had planned the entire rebuilding of the Schools Quad-rangle with three storeys, the topmost being reserved for the library, which he foresaw as growing steadily after his death.

Building work began, it is said, on the day of Bodley's funeral in 1613, and was completed in 1624. The austerity of this quadrangle is relieved by the

The frontispiece, King James I.

magnificent frontispiece of the five orders of classical architecture, with statuary portraying King James I giving his works to the University, on his left, and to Fame wielding her trumpet.

In 1636 William Laud, Archbishop of Canterbury and Chancellor of the University, added a west wing which changed the ground plan of the library from T to H. It was named after John Selden who gave to the University his library of some eight thousand books and valuable oriental manuscripts. Today the Bodleian occupies the whole of the Old Schools Quadrangle, including the magnificent Divinity School hall below Duke Humfrey's Library, and also the Radcliffe Camera and the "New Bodleian" on the other side of Broad Street; both of these are connected with the central buildings by underground galleries containing some eighty-five miles (135km.) of shelving and many of the Library's six million volumes and extensive collections of maps, manuscripts, and incunabula.

Each of the thirty-nine colleges and virtually every Faculty and Department has its own library – some very large, some highly specialized – to all of which the Bodleian has access through what is claimed to be the largest academic library system in the world.

Duke Humfrey's Library.

THE BOTANIC GARDEN

The plot of land was in use as a Jewish cemetery from about 1190 until the expulsion of the Jews in 1290. The plot was abandoned until 1620, when Henry Danvers, Earl of Danby, bought it from Magdalen and established a herbarium or "Physick Garden" for the Faculty of Medicine, one of the oldest herb gardens in Europe. He built the boundary wall and the magnificent gateway, and he endowed the garden with a Keeper; this was an eccentric German named Jacob Bobart, who collected a vast number of plants and seeds from all over Europe – including, from the slopes of Mount Etna, the "Ragwort" which later escaped from the garden and spread all over England. Botany gained importance as a study distinct from medicine; by the beginning of the 19th century the two subjects were separate, and in 1840 the "evolutionist" Professor Charles Daubeny adopted the name Botanic Garden and encouraged studies in botanical evolution; in 1848 he built a laboratory here at his own expense.

Professor Daubeny was chairman of the meeting of the British Association held in June 1860 to discuss Charles Darwin's theories, and it was at the Botanic Garden that the "evolutionists" celebrated Thomas Huxley's famous debating victory over the "creationist" Samuel Wilberforce, Bishop of Oxford.

The rock garden.

Inside a glass-house where a water lily is named after Charles Daubeny.

BRASENOSE COLLEGE

Radcliffe Square front.

Brasenose College was founded in 1509 by two northerners from the Cheshire-Lancashire border – Bishop William Smyth, and Richard Sutton, a lawyer and the first layman spontaneously to found a college. The buildings were put up on the site of several medieval halls, including Brazen Nose Hall, so called for the bronze knocker or sanctuary ring on the door. In the riots of 1334 there was an exodus from Oxford, in which the scholars of Brazen Nose Hall migrated to Stamford in Lincolnshire, taking the Nose with them.

It remained there when the scholars returned to Oxford a few years later, and was recovered only in 1890. Today the Nose may be seen behind the high table in the dining hall; the nose above the main gate was carved for the opening of the college. The front, (Old) quadrangle, a good example of Tudor domestic architecture, dates from 1509, except for the top floor dormer windows added a century later. There is a complicated sun-dial dated 1719.

Old Quad.

CHRIST CHURCH – *The House*

Tom Tower.

The House had its origins in a grandiose scheme conceived in the 1520s by Cardinal Thomas Wolsey: his "Cardinal College" was to excel all others in its edifices and by its intellectual supremacy. He succeeded in building the dining hall – then the largest in England – the kitchen, and part of the Great Quadrangle; but in 1529 he fell out of favour with Henry VIII and the scheme was halted. The King in 1532 took over Wolsey's beginning and set it on its feet as King Henry VIII College. Then in 1546 he refounded it on more ambitious lines as The House of Christ in Oxford, and he appointed the Dean and Chapter of the newly established Cathedral as the governing body of "The House", as it is commonly called. Wolsey's Great Quadrangle remained half-built and was not completed until the 1660s; Tom Tower above the gatehouse, built in 1682 by Christopher Wren, houses the bell "Great Tom", from Oseney Abbey, which has given its name not only to the tower where it hangs but also to the Great Quadrangle, "Tom Quad".

Hall and Meadow Building.

Peckwater Quad and Library.

Library interior and Merton College Tower.

CHRIST CHURCH – *The Cathedral*

The Chancel.

The Cathedral was originally the church of the Augustinian Priory of St Frideswide; it was built 1160–75 on the site of St Frideswide's chapel of, probably, about AD 720. The Priory was suppressed by Cardinal Wolsey, and after the Diocese of Oxford was created in 1542 Henry VIII designated St Frideswide's church as the Cathedral and renamed it The Church of Christ in Oxford. This church, besides being the Cathedral, also serves as the chapel of King Henry's "House".

Christ Church is well known world-wide for its choir who, besides their normal duties, have made many broadcasts and recordings of both liturgical and secular music, and have travelled widely. Architecturally the Cathedral has many interesting peculiarities; the structure is mainly mid-12th-century, and therefore Norman in style, but there is a superb Perpendicular vault of about 1500 over the chancel, attributed to William Orchard who made the vaulting of the Divinity School.

The Cathedral spire over Tom Quad, with Mercury fountain.

THE CLARENDON BUILDING

Edward Hyde, first Earl of Clarendon (1609–1674), a staunch Royalist in the Civil War, was Chancellor of the University in 1660–67. After the Restoration of the Monarchy he wrote the *History of the Rebellion and Wars in England* the copyright of which he bequeathed to the University. The book proved to be the best seller of the time and the proceeds in part financed a new building for the University Press, which was outgrowing the cellars and attics of the Sheldonian Theatre, where it had begun its existence.

The neo-classical Clarendon Building (1711–13) is the work of Nicholas Hawksmoor, and is said to be derived from a sketch by John Vanbrugh – with whom Hawksmoor was working at Blenheim Palace, Woodstock. The Press moved into its new quarters in 1713 and began to use the Clarendon imprint, which it has retained despite moving again in 1830 to Walton Street. The building is now largely given over to Proctors' offices and other administrative purposes.

The Sheldonian Theatre and the Clarendon Building.

CORPUS CHRISTI COLLEGE

Front Quad and Pelican Column.

"Corpus", 1517, the last pre-Reformation college, was founded by Bishop Richard Fox, one of the last ecclesiastical benefactors in the old tradition. However, he was no traditionalist and he intended that his college should instruct secular clergy in the "New Learning" of the Renaissance – that is, the classical humanities. He established Oxford's first lectureship in Greek, and he set up in the college a trilingual library of Latin, Greek, and Hebrew classics, much admired by Erasmus. Bishop Fox was a fanciful man and saw the Fellows and scholars as busy bees collecting the honey of learning; it is said that in the 1520s a colony of bees settled in the roof and continued to be active until the Puritan Visitation of 1648. In the Civil War, Corpus managed to avoid surrendering its silver treasures to the Royal Mint, and so today possesses the finest collection of plate in Oxford, including Bishop Fox's pastoral crosier. The Pelican, the college's emblem taken from the coat of arms of Bishop Fox, symbolizes the Body of Christ.

The Fellows' Garden.

EXETER COLLEGE

The Chapel.

This is the fourth oldest college in Oxford, founded in 1314 by Walter Stapledon, Bishop of Exeter. The college was poorly endowed and its early years were penurious. A timely benefactor was Sir William Petre, who in 1566 retired as Secretary of State under Queen Elizabeth I after amassing a large fortune over many years' service during four reigns. Among his benefactions was the bequest of his library, which included the 14th-century illuminated Bohun Psalter. In the 19th century Exeter was in a sense the cradle of the PreRaphaelite movement; William Morris and Edward Burne-Jones were undergraduates together here when they first met Dante Gabriel Rosetti. A tapestry made by Morris after a painting by Burne-Jones, The Adoration of the Magi, hangs in the chapel. The only medieval building is Palmer's Tower, now part of the Rector's Lodging; this was the original gatehouse on the lane that ran inside the city wall and it was the entrance to the college until the Turl Street front was built in 1703.

44

The Library and the Fellows' Garden.

The Hall

The Fellows' Garden.

GREEN COLLEGE

Lankester Quad.

This is one of the more recently founded of Oxford's colleges; it owes its existence to Dr Cecil Green, head of Texas Instruments Inc., who in 1977 made a substantial gift to the University to set up a graduate college for clinical medical students and tutors, and those working in related disciplines. The new buildings forming the front quadrangle, completed in 1979, are in a modest domestic style designed by the University Surveyor, Jack Lankester; they avoid competition with the college's outstanding feature. The Radcliffe Observatory with its Tower of Winds, built between 1772 and 1794, was one of the bequests of Dr John Radcliffe and is among Oxford's most distinguished buildings. Nikolaus Pevsner says it is "architecturally the finest observatory of Europe", and Oxford has reason to be glad that it has been fully restored by Green College.

Radcliffe Observatory; the Tower of Winds.

HARRIS–MANCHESTER COLLEGE

The formal name of this establishment is The Manchester Academy and Harris College. It was founded in Manchester in 1786 and, after several moves, came to Oxford in 1889. It is a theological college offering courses in the liberal arts as well as training for the Nonconformist ministry. In 1996, with the financial support of Lord Harris of Peckham, it was fully integrated in the University and became the thirty-ninth federated college. This, it is thought, will be appreciated by the many theology students from the U.S.A. who customarily complete their courses with a year at Manchester in Oxford. The college can now present its members for matriculation and graduation by the University.

HERTFORD COLLEGE

The Front Quad.

Hertford's history begins with Hart Hall, set up in the 1280s as an academic hall and acquiring some importance – even possessing its own library. In 1740 the energetic Principal, Dr Richard Newton, refounded the hall as Hertford College. Despite the paucity of its endowments, it was successful during Dr Newton's lifetime and for some years afterwards, but in 1775 it began slowly to decline, until by 1805 there were no students and only one Fellow. In 1818 the college was closed; in 1820 the medieval Catte Street front collapsed; but in 1822 the buildings were reopened, to be occupied by Magdalen Hall who rebuilt the Catte Street front and renamed the place. The enterprise flourished; in 1868 the vigorous Dr Michell became Principal and, with a generous endowment from the banker Thomas Baring, refounded it in 1874 as Hertford College.

Most of Hertford College, including the well-known "Bridge of Sighs", is by Thomas Jackson.

Jackson's staircase to the hall.

The Principal's Lodgings.

Jesus is generally known as the Welsh College. Hugh Price, the Founder under Queen Elizabeth's patronage, was Treasurer of St David's Cathedral, Pembroke, who had been schooled at Oxford and wished to provide an Oxford house for Welsh scholars. Jesus College was built on the site of the medieval White Hall in Turl Street. Progress was slow because Hugh Price, who was 76 when he made the foundation in 1571, died three years later without having secured adequate endowments.

The college prospered between 1613 and the Civil War under a succession of three energetic Principals who attracted benefactions and completed the Founder's plans. After the Commonwealth the college – which had remained Royalist – was again impoverished, but in 1661 the influential Sir Leoline Jenkins became Principal and presided over its recovery. He later became Secretary of State and in 1685 died bequeathing his large fortune to the college.

Gateway.

First Quad.

Inner Quad.

KEBLE COLLEGE

Parks Road Front.

Keble College was set up by the Tractarians, the leaders of the Oxford Movement, partly as a memorial to John Keble, one of the founders of the Movement, and partly in response to the perceived lack of opportunities at Oxford for poor students – stressed by Keble himself. There was no rich benefactor and no government help, but on Keble's death in 1866 the Archbishop of Canterbury launched an appeal for public subscriptions. The appeal was remarkably successful; the foundation stone of the college was laid only two years later, and by 1870 the first buildings were in use. If the founding Tractarians had had their way, this would have been a theological college; but the first Warden, Edward Talbot, had other ideas and opened the college to all comers. The buildings of Keble, by William Butterfield – himself a supporter of the Oxford Movement – are all in red brick with ornamentation in brick of other colours; they are hardly less controversial today than when they were first constructed.

The Chapel, Front Quad and Oxford.

LADY MARGARET HALL

Talbot Hall and gardens.

This was the first residential hall for women, and was for members of the Church of England only. It was founded in 1878 by the inspiring Dame Elizabeth Wordsworth and her friends in the Association for the Education of Women in Oxford, and named after Lady Margaret Beaufort, the mother of Henry VII and a benefactress of Oxford. L.M.H. became an independent self-governing institution in 1953 and acquired full college status in the University in 1959, but did not change its name. In the centenary year of its opening, 1979, the college admitted men as Fellows and as undergraduates, and a man was appointed Principal. Architecturally L.M.H. is largely built in pleasant red-brick country-house style, with designs by Basil Champneys and Reginald Blomfield, and in the 20th century Giles Gilbert Scott and others. The group is enhanced by its fine position on the Cherwell.

Encaenia Garden Party in the College grounds.

LINACRE COLLEGE

Linacre House was set up by the University in 1962 to provide social amenities for "unattached" graduates from other universities staying in Oxford to read for further degrees. The initial concept was a non-residential centre with common rooms and dining rights – a sort of club-house – and it was housed in the Worthington Building in St Aldate's. The experiment revealed that visiting graduates also needed living accommodation. In 1964 Linacre became a college, and in 1977 it moved to a house named Cherwell Edge, which was enlarged to provide the desired residential quarters; in 1986 Linacre acquired full collegiate status with its membership confined to visiting graduates.

LINCOLN COLLEGE

The Hall.

Lincoln is the eighth college foundation, set up in 1427 by Richard Fleming, Bishop of Lincoln (the Diocese then included Oxford) with the purpose of teaching young priests to combat heresies and to defend the true faith and the mysteries of Scripture. Bishop Fleming was unable to achieve sufficient resources but his successor as Bishop of Lincoln, Thomas Rotherham, secured new endowments and in 1479 gave the college its statutes, for which he is acknowledged as the Second Founder.

The college can claim to be the birthplace of the Methodist Church since John Wesley, who was a Fellow in the years 1726–51, used to hold in college meetings of The Holy Club founded by him and his brother Charles. The college has been able to compensate for its restricted site by acquiring the church of All Saints, designed probably by Dean Henry Aldrich assisted by Hawksmoor, built in 1706–8. It has been very successfully converted into the library.

Front Quad.

The Library (All Saints Church).

MAGDALEN COLLEGE

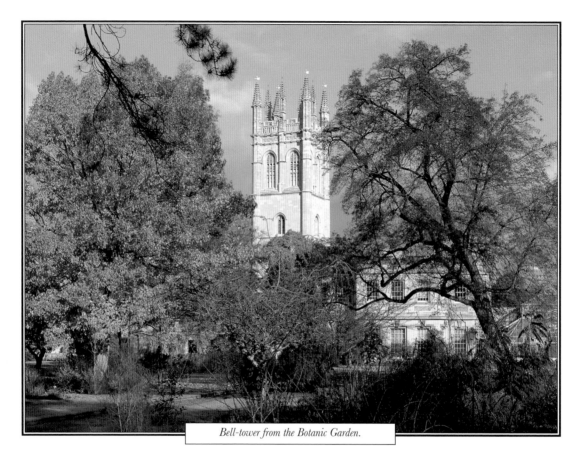

Bell-tower from the Botanic Garden.

Physically Magdalen is one of the most attractive colleges, with its impressive buildings and deer park in their riverside setting. Chronologically it is the tenth foundation; and financially it is one of the richest. William of Wayneflete (1395–1486), Bishop of Winchester and Lord Chancellor under Henry VI, was a rich and powerful churchman in the medieval tradition. He had possibly been a scholar at New College and seems to have followed the same road as William of Wykeham.

Wayneflete in 1458 received from the King the 13th-century Hospital of St John the Baptist, outside the East Gate of the city. This foundation owned lands and revenues that provided an ample site and generous endowments for Wayneflete's college. His plans were delayed until 1474 by the Wars of the Roses, but he was tenacious and long-lived, and at the age of 91 he saw the completion of all his buildings except the bell-tower, which was begun in 1492 and completed in 1509 probably by William Orchard.

The Rose Garden.

The New Buildings (1733).

The Bell-tower and the River Cherwell.

MANSFIELD COLLEGE

The setting up of Mansfield College was the outcome of a decision made in 1886 by the Congregational Churches in response to the opening up of Oxford University to Nonconformists. The Free Churches moved their Spring Hill College – a theological college – from Birmingham to Oxford, where it was renamed after the original founders. Here it continued its theological studies and training for the ministry as well as encouraging other students. Mansfield became a Permanent Private Hall in 1955, and in 1995 became the thirty-eighth fully integrated college. Today the majority, graduate and undergraduate, are not pursuing theological studies but reading secular subjects. The college buildings, completed in 1889, are in the best "college gothic" of Basil Champneys, who gave Oxford several notable buildings.

The Hall.

MERTON COLLEGE

Merton is one of the three earliest foundations in Oxford, and was the first to receive statutes as a college in 1264. Walter de Merton was Lord Chancellor under Henry III and was later Bishop of Rochester – a rich and influential churchman of the kind that governed England in the Middle Ages. His aim, in the tradition of his day, was the training of secular priests to be competent administrators of Church and State. He was opposed to the monastic and mendicant orders for their obstruction of the advance in learning, and his college statutes expressly forbade members to make any monastic vows, on pain of expulsion. The college became prominent in the 14th century for its progressive thinking, but was not without accusations of heresy when John Wycliffe was a member. In later centuries Merton led the advances in astronomy, mathematics, and medicine, and was noted for the Warden Sir Henry Savile who in 1619 founded the Savilian Chairs of Geometry and Astronomy.

Fellows' Garden before the limes were felled.

Grove Building, Meadow front.

Chapel Tower.

NEW COLLEGE

Garden Quad.

William of Wykeham's foundation, St Mary College of Winchester in Oxford, the seventh in seniority, 1379, came to be called New College to distinguish it from the older House of the Blessed Mary the Virgin, known as Oriel College. William of Wykeham, Bishop of Winchester and Lord Chancellor to Edward III, was probably the richest man in England. He set out to provide for the education of secular priests as ministers of Church and State, and to open up careers for his many nephews. His grammar school in Winchester ensured a supply of scholars adequately prepared for a university education, New College provided it, and the system achieved a high academic standard; still today "Wykehamists" are academically well regarded. New College was noted in recent times for its Warden (1903–25) Dr W. A. Spooner, the scholarly eccentric who unwittingly lent his name to spoonerisms such as: "Who does not have in his heart a half-warmed fish ..." or "You have hissed all my mystery lectures".

The Great Quad and central Oxford.

The Cloister.

The eighteenth-century wrought iron screen with the garden beyond.

NUFFIELD COLLEGE

The college was founded in 1937 when "Bill" Morris, Viscount Nuffield, offered the University one million pounds to set up a college on the site that he had bought near the Castle. He was persuaded that the college should be for social research, though he had little sympathy with sociologists. Building work on the site was delayed by disagreements until it was ruled out by war in 1939; the college had meanwhile come into existence and its members worked in temporary premises. Building was begun in 1949 and completed in 1960; Lord Nuffield criticized the University over the slowness of progress – both academic and architectural – but he was satisfied when his foundation acquired full collegiate status in 1958; when he died in 1963 he had bequeathed to the college the remainder of his substantial fortune. As a research college, Nuffield does no teaching and it admits only graduates. It was one of the first colleges open to women as well as men.

The College Spire over the Oxford Canal.

ORIEL COLLEGE

The House of the Blessed Mary the Virgin in Oxford,1326, was the fifth foundation. Adam de Brome, Rector of the University Church of St Mary the Virgin, obtained the consent of Edward II to diverting the church revenues to the founding of a college, the King being named as founder. Adam de Brome was successful in attracting endowments, including the royal gift of St Bartholomew's Hospital for lepers off the Cowley Road, where the chapel, almshouses and a farm-house have been restored.

Oriel became prominent in the early 19th century as the home of the Oxford Movement (the Tractarians) when John Keble, John Henry Newman, and Thomas Arnold were Fellows and counted among their supporters the noted Canon Edward Pusey of Christ Church. To a long tradition of academic excellence, Oriel has in more recent years added pre-eminence in rowing: it has been Head of the River for more consecutive years than any other college.

The buildings of the Front Quad include the hall, chapel, and portico of 1620–40.

St Mary's Quad containing remnants of the medieval St Mary's Hall.

Back Quad.

PEMBROKE COLLEGE

The Hall, 1848.

The college was founded in 1624 nominally by James I, though he gave only Letters Patent and permission to use his name. The real founders were two rich citizens of Abingdon who wished to make a university education accessible to their kin and to the boys of Abingdon Grammar School. The college was named after the third Earl of Pembroke, who was Chancellor of the University at the time, and who was expected to make a substantial benefaction; unfortunately he died in 1630 without doing so. Charles I, however, gave the college two important endowments. The founders acquired Broadgates Hall and other adjoining medieval halls and in 1888 bought from Christ Church a group of almshouses built by Cardinal Wolsey in 1525, which now form Pembroke's street front on St Aldate's. Pembroke is noted for having put up with the unruly, abrasive, indigent Samuel Johnson for four terms in 1728–9. He did not graduate but always remembered Oxford appreciatively.

The Gate-tower.

Old Quad.

Chapel Quad, the plain exterior of the 1732 chapel conceals a richly decorated baroque interior.

QUEEN'S COLLEGE

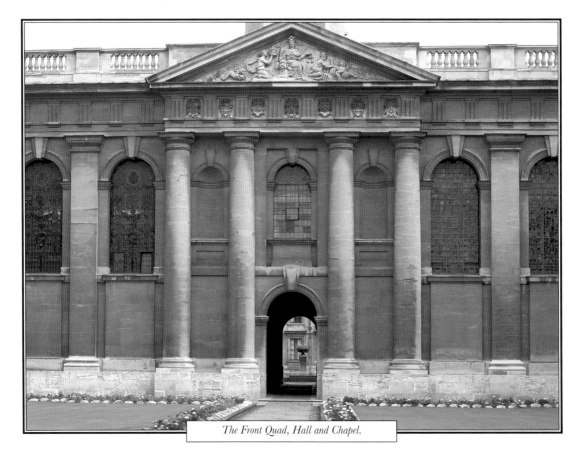

The Front Quad, Hall and Chapel.

Also called The Queen's College, this was Oxford's sixth foundation, in 1341; Robert de Eglesfield was a Cumberland man, chaplain to Queen Philippa (consort of Edward III) with whose patronage and help he was able to set up a house for scholars and "Poor Boys" from Cumberland and Westmorland. Subsequent royal consorts extended their patronage to the foundation, including Queen Caroline (George III) whose statue stands beneath the cupola above the main gate on the High Street.

Eglesfield's unusual statutes provide for a Provost and twelve Fellows, who were to seat themselves at the dinner table as in paintings of The Last Supper, with the Provost on a throne. The Fellows were to be summoned to dinner by a trumpet call, as they still are on special occasions. Queen's was the last college to cease brewing its own beer, and the old brew-house may be seen at the end of a picturesque alley to the west of the Front Quad, leading to Nun's Garden.

Front Quad with the Cupola.

The Library.

Lane to Nun's Garden and the old brewhouse.

THE RADCLIFFE CAMERA

This most distinctive of Oxford landmarks is described by Nikolaus Pevsner as "England's most accomplished domed building", and indeed many people see in it a calm elegance that sets it apart from its largely Jacobean surroundings. Dr John Radcliffe, a Univ man from Yorkshire, physician to William III, to Queen Anne, and to a circle of rich admirers in London, died in 1714 bequeathing to the University his great collection of scientific books, and funds to build a library to house them.

A rotunda design was submitted by Nicholas Hawksmoor and accepted by the University, but building work was delayed until 1737 by negotiations to clear the crowded site. Hawksmoor died in 1736, and the work was entrusted to James Gibbs. Later Dr Radcliffe's books were moved to The John Radcliffe Science Library in Parks Road, and the Camera then became one of the reading rooms of the Bodleian Library, with which it is connected by an underground tunnel.

Interior of dome.

"All bad lots", a window below the dome.

REWLEY HOUSE & KELLOGG COLLEGE

The Courtyard.

Rewley House is the recently modernized group of buildings at the entrance to Wellington Square, housing both the Department for Continuing Education and Kellogg College. Inside the Victorian facade are a lecture theatre, library, dining room, seminar rooms, offices and study-bedrooms. The Department gives non-traditional students access to the academic standards of Oxford. Kellogg College is the base for part-time degree students at the University. It was opened in 1990 as Rewley House, and renamed Kellogg College in October 1994 in recognition of generous benefactions from the W.K. Kellogg Foundation. The College is the thirty-sixth house to be federated with the University.

SAID BUSINESS SCHOOL

Front from the south west

Established in 1996 the Saïd Business School is an integral part of the University. The school is developing a new generation of business leaders and entrepreneurs and conducts research not only into the nature of business, but the connections between business and the wider world.

The school's newest building opened in October 2001 and was designed by the architects Dixon and Jones.

ST ANNE'S COLLEGE

The college began as the Society of Home Students, founded in 1890 by the Association for the Education of Women in Oxford (A.E.W.) as an academic vehicle for young women living in Oxford and wanting university-level schooling – dons' daughters for example. The Society's first home was in the private house of the first Principal, Mrs Bertha Johnson; by the 1920s the students were increasing in numbers and membership was no longer confined to Oxford residents. The 1930s brought several benefactions that enabled the Society to acquire its present large site between Woodstock and Banbury Roads, where several buildings have been put up. The Society became St Anne's College by incorporation in 1952, and it achieved full college status in 1959. In 1978 the statutes were changed to admit men, who now account for about half the college membership.

ST ANTONY'S COLLEGE

The foundation derives from a gift to the University made by a French business-man, M. Antonin Besse, to promote international relations. Though the gift was offered in 1948 it was not until 1950 that the college actually came into being; it received its charter in 1953 and acquired full college status in 1965. The college admits graduates only, women and men, and as intended by the founder the members are largely occupied in the study of other countries and regions. The college also receives visiting Fellows and graduate students from all parts of the world. St Antony's is housed in a 19th-century Gothic convent building and a modern, 1970s, block containing the hall and common rooms.

St Catherine's College

St Catherine's Society was the name adopted in 1931 by the movement started by the University in the 1860s to help "unattached" or "non-collegiate" students to gain access to university tuition without the expense of college membership. The numbers of such students increased, while the legislation introduced in 1944 made college membership open to all students and did away with the reasons for students being "non-collegiate". By the early 1950s there were enough undergraduate members of St Catherine's Society to constitute a residential college; accordingly a large site in Holywell Great Meadow was acquired in 1957, and with energetic fund-raising St Catherine's College was built – to designs by Arne Jacobsen – and opened in 1964. By 1978 it had become Oxford's largest college, with academic and sporting achievements of distinction. It was one of the first men's colleges to welcome women. and has succeeded in being a modern institution without abandoning any of Oxford's deeply rooted principles.

West face of Great Quad.

A corner of the garden.

ST CROSS COLLEGE

St Cross was founded by the University in 1965 to provide fellowships for academic staff appointed by the University – the "non-dons" – and college membership for some of the growing number of graduate students. The college began very modestly in an old school house and a wooden hut near St Cross Church; in 1981 it moved to its present site in St Giles, which it shares with Pusey House. Since the move various improvements and additions have been carried out in the buildings with the help of grants from other Oxford colleges and some generous benefactions. The buildings, facilities and student numbers have almost doubled in recent years, but the College plans to remain comparatively small.

The Four Colleges Arch and the Richard Blackwell Quadrangle.

St Edmund Hall

Gateway.

St Edmund Hall ("Teddy Hall") has existed as an academic entity since the 1190s when St Edmund Riche of Abingdon lived and taught in a hall on this site. Little is known of its very early history, but in 1270 it was owned and maintained by Oseney Abbey; at the Dissolution of the Monasteries in 1539 the hall escaped being dissolved but was left in a precarious state for several years until in 1557 it was bought by the Provost of Queen's College. It then became a subsidiary of Queen's, with a Principal appointed by the college, but no Fellows. Teddy Hall was never absorbed by Queen's, but it continued a semi-independent existence under the tutelage of the college, gradually increasing its autonomy until in 1957 it achieved full college status, but did not change its name. From these modest beginnings St Edmund Hall has become numerically one of Oxford's largest houses.

Front Quad.

St Hilda's College

St Hilda's South.

Miss Dorothea Beale, the Principal of Cheltenham Ladies' College, bought Cowley House, a late 18th-century mansion on a fine site beside the River Cherwell, and in 1893 set up a hall primarily for Cheltenham girls, with her school colleague Mrs Esther Burrows as Principal.

After a modest beginning with limited financial resources, St Hilda's Hall acquired new vigour under Miss Julia de Lacy Mann, Principal 1928–55, whose strong personality stimulated its growth. The Hall became St Hilda's College in 1926, and in 1959 it obtained full college status in the University, at the same time as the other women's colleges.

Adjoining properties have been bought and several buildings have been put up on what is now an extensive site, including the Jaqueline du Pre music building. The college has had its own boathouse and complement of punts since soon after its foundation.

Buildings on the Cherwell.

ST HUGH'S COLLEGE

Main Buildings.

This is a second foundation (1886) of Dame Elizabeth Wordsworth, who intended it as an economical alternative to Lady Margaret Hall for the less affluent. St Hugh's began modestly in an ordinary house in North Oxford; under the first Principal, Miss Anne Moberly, the venture grew rapidly in numbers and prominence, and in 1913 was able to acquire its present ample site, which contains buildings of various years from 1916 to 1992; it was the first of the women's colleges to occupy its own specifically designed building. The site also embraces several acres of gardens created and tended for many years by Miss Annie Rogers, an eminent classicist and a keen follower of the noted gardener Gertrude Jekyll. St Hugh's obtained full college status in 1959, admitted men tutors in 1977, male undergraduates in 1987, and now has a man as Principal.

Gardens from the South.

ST JOHN'S COLLEGE

The Gate-tower.

The Founder was Sir Thomas White, a rich member of the Merchant Taylors' Company and an Alderman and Lord Mayor of London; in 1555 he acquired the site and buildings of St Bernard's College, a dissolved Cistercian House. He was a Roman Catholic and his college was intended to combat the Protestant heresies as well as to further the education of boys from the Merchant Taylors' School. In the 17th century St John's benefited from the generosity of its most eminent member: William Laud was a scholar, then a Fellow, and later President, of the college, Chancellor of the University, Bishop of Bath & Wells and of London, and Archbishop of Canterbury; he reformed the University statutes with his Laudian Code of 1636, and in the same year he gave his college the magnificent Canterbury Quad, which Pevsner calls "a princely job".

Garden front of Laud's buildings.

Canterbury Quad. Laud received King Charles and Queen Henrietta Maria here,
and it is said that the entertainment cost nearly as much as the buildings.

The garden.

THE CHURCH OF ST MARY THE VIRGIN

St Mary's Church is historically the most important building in Oxford; there has been a church on the site since Saxon times, and in age St Mary's surpasses its surroundings by half a millennium. The huge tower and spire still dominate central Oxford much as the powerful University – a Church institution – dominated the citizens of the town in the Middle Ages.

From the earliest days the Masters used St Mary's for sessions of the Chancellor's Court, for disputations and trials for heresy – such as those of the three Protestant Bishops condemned and martyred in Oxford – for many secular ceremonies and celebrations including the boisterous "Act" (later Encaenia), and as a general meeting place for Masters. St Mary's became known as the University Church, although the University has never had any official rights in it.

Many notable divines have preached from St Mary's pulpit, including John Wesley and John Henry Newman who was Vicar of the parish in 1828-43 until he "went over to Rome". The University Sermon, on Sundays during term-time, is often preached at St Mary's. Over the years the University has acquired its own buildings for academic, legal, and celebratory purposes, and its reliance on St Mary's

The Baroque Portico.

has dwindled to the weekly sermon and an occasional special service.

The massive tower, antedating all but the three oldest colleges, was built about 1300 adjoining the 11th-century nave, as it then was, and the spire was added some twenty years later. The choir and the nave were rebuilt between the 1460s and 1490s and are, with modifications, what stands today. The baroque portico over the south door on the High Street was the gift of Archbishop Laud and his chaplain, designed and built by Nicholas Stone in 1637.

The old Congregation House at the north-east corner of St Mary's was given to the University in 1320 by Thomas Cobham, Bishop of Winchester; it provided an upper floor to house his legacy of books – the beginnings of the University library – and a council chamber below. In the 1480s the books were moved to Duke Humfrey's Library and the space was used for archives. Congregation continued to meet in the lower hall until the Convocation House was built in 1637. Since then the building has been put to many uses, including that of a garage for the university fire engine. A meeting held there in October 1942 set up the Oxford Committee for Famine Relief (OXFAM).

The High Street front.

ST PETER'S COLLEGE

St Peter's occupies the site of the ancient New Inn Hall. In 1874 the parish church of St Peter-le-Bailey was moved from inside the Castle bailey and rebuilt close to New Inn Hall and to an 18th-century building formerly used by the Oxford Canal Company. The Rector of the parish, the Revd. Henry Linton, bought this building to serve as his rectory. A later Rector, the Revd. Christopher Chavasse, with financial help from Lord Nuffield, in 1929 bought the New Inn Hall buildings, added his rectory, and refounded the amalgam as St Peter's Hall; when the parish church of St Peter was made redundant it became the college chapel. In 1961 the Hall acquired full collegiate status and changed its name accordingly. With the help of benefactors, including Lord Nuffield and Antonin Besse, the college has bought and integrated several adjoining buildings, in step with its growth.

Doorway to Morris Building.

THE SHELDONIAN THEATRE

Christopher Wren, a Fellow of All Souls, was commissioned by Gilbert Sheldon, Archbishop of Canterbury and Chancellor of the University, to design an assembly hall for the secular and sometimes rowdy ceremonies, such as "The Act", now *Encaenia*, that were still being held in St Mary's Church. This was in 1663; Wren was aged 31 and the theatre was his first public building.

Wren's design was inspired by the open-air Theatre of Marcellus in Rome, and is also on a D-shaped ground plan. Because of its principal ceremonial purpose, the front of the Sheldonian faces the Divinity School and it is the curved back that is seen from Broad Street.

Old prints show Wren's original design had large oval dormer windows giving light to the wide roof-space, which along with other parts of the building was used by the early printing works that later became the University Press and issued books with the imprint of the Theatre. The roof of the Theatre was rebuilt in 1802, without the dormer windows, and in 1838 Wren's lantern was replaced by a larger and heavier design by Edward Blore.

In pursuit of an open-air illusion Wren contrived an unsupported flat ceiling – at 70ft. by 80ft. the widest in its day – painted to represent the sky

The Chancellor's Throne.

and including the ropes and canopy that in a Roman theatre would have shaded the audience. The painting, an elaborate allegorical scene by Robert Streater, was brought in thirty-two panels from his London studio to Oxford by Thames barge. In the centre of the auditorium is the gilded Chancellor's throne, and at the sides are the two Proctors' boxes ornamented with fasces symbolizing proctorial authority.

The so-called "Emperors", the fourteen carved stone heads on columns standing on Broad Street are thought not to be emperors, nor philosophers, but simply Wren's version of the boundary stones surmounted by heads as seen in Rome. The present heads are the third set, by the Oxford sculptor Michael Black, put up in 1972 to replace the badly eroded 1867 set, which had replaced the originals.

The Sheldonian is not suitable for staging drama and has only rarely been used for the purpose, but it has served as Oxford's principal concert hall since before 1733 when Handel spent a week in Oxford conducting performances of his works, including the first of his new oratorio Athalia. Haydn's Symphony No 92 in G was played here in 1791 and has been known ever since then as the "Oxford" Symphony.

The Encaenia Ceremony when honorary degrees are conferred.

The Broad Street aspect.

SOMERVILLE COLLEGE

This is the non-denominational response to the Anglican Lady Margaret Hall and is similarly the creation of the Association for the Education of Women. Set up in 1879 as a residential hall for women, its founders asserted their detachment from religious considerations by naming the house after Mary Somerville (1780–1872), one of the most eminent scientists of her day. The title of "college" was adopted in 1894 to indicate the governing body's intentions. Somerville achieved full independent college status in 1959, but it delayed until 1993 the decision to admit men.

The Garden Quad and Library.

TEMPLETON COLLEGE

This graduate foundation had its beginnings in the Oxford Centre for Management Studies, which was set up in 1965 on a site in Kennington given by Mr Clifford Barclay. In 1984 a substantial benefaction from Sir John Templeton enabled the Centre to develop its activities. Templeton acquired its Royal Charter in 1995 and became Oxford's thirty-seventh federated college and its designated centre for executive education.

TRINITY COLLEGE

Chapel and old Gate-tower.

Trinity stands on the site of the medieval Durham College, dissolved in 1539. The buildings were bought in 1555 by Sir Thomas Pope, an Oxfordshire lawyer who had amassed a fortune in the service of Henry VIII. After a slow beginning Trinity progressed when Ralph Kettell became President in 1599; he improved the college's academic status and its finances, and he built a new hall to replace the old one, which had collapsed. He was eccentric but much liked. After an interval he was followed by his equally vigorous grandson Ralph Bathurst, who became President in 1664 and continued the work that Dr Kettell had begun. Bathurst was a friend of Christopher Wren, and they were both members of the group of Oxford and Cambridge scientists who, with John Wilkins of Wadham College, founded the Royal Society in London in 1662.

Front Quad, the Jackson Building.

The chapel of 1692, a neo-classical design attributed to Dean Henry Aldrich, assisted by Christopher Wren.

Garden Quad.

UNIVERSITY COLLEGE

Master's Lodgings and Radcliffe Quad.

"Univ" is one of the three oldest colleges; the bequest on which it was founded was made by William, Archdeacon of Durham, who died in 1249 leaving a legacy for the University to set up a house for ten Masters. This small community came into existence soon afterwards, but it did not receive statutes to establish it as a college until 1280, and it did not occupy buildings of its own until 1331, eighty-two years after the founding bequest. The college prospered little until after the Reformation; in the 17th century it received several benefactions, notably one from Dr John Radcliffe – a Univ man – which financed the building of the Radcliffe Quad in 1716. Obadiah Walker, who was Bursar at the time of the Civil War and Master in 1676–89, was a successful fund-raiser for the college, but in the reign of James II he was converted to Roman Catholicism and set up a Catholic chapel in the college. He was eventually deposed from the mastership when James lost the throne in the Revolution of 1688.

Radcliffe Quad gateway, fan vaulting.

Chapel glass by Abraham van Linge: Adam and Eve lamenting their lot.

The Hall, largely seventeenth-century.

THE UNIVERSITY MUSEUM

A museum of natural history, equipped with lecture-rooms and laboratories, as a centre for the teaching of all branches of science was first thought of in 1848 by Sir Henry Acland, an eminent physician and Regius Professor of Medicine from 1857 to 1894. The museum, completed in 1860, is remarkable for the fine iron-work and glazing of its interior structure, which Acland described as "railway materials". Soon after the building was completed several departments of the science Faculties moved in from their widely scattered quarters in the town, thus fulfilling Acland's aims. The museum building was soon fully occupied and auxiliary buildings were put up. In this way the Science Area came into being with its centre at the University Museum, which contained in one place all the collections of scientific material made since Elias Ashmole's time. Adjoining the University Museum is the renowned Pitt Rivers Museum of anthropology and ethnology, and the Balfour Library.

Acland's "railway materials", and museum displays.

WADHAM COLLEGE

Front Quad frontispiece.

The college was founded by Nicholas Wadham and his wife Dorothy, of Merifield in Somerset, rich landed gentry with no heirs. Nicholas died in 1609 before anything tangible had been done, and it was Dorothy, by then in her seventies, who carried out his intentions. She engaged the Merifield architect-stonemason William Arnold as her factotum; Dorothy herself never came to Oxford, but directed the whole operation from home through the highly competent Arnold. Astonishingly, the whole college was built in three years,

1610–13, and the Warden and Fellows moved in at once. Dorothy drew up the statutes and appointed all members of the college, including the servants. The college was much disrupted by the Civil War, but the Warden appointed by the Parliamentarian government in 1648, John Wilkins, was not only married to Oliver Cromwell's sister, but was also an eminent astronomer and scientist. He attracted other scientists, and the group contributed to the foundation of the Royal Society in London in 1662.

South Front and Garden.

The Hall.

Dorothy Wadham.

WOLFSON COLLEGE

This foundation by the University in 1965 was at first named Iffley College; its purpose was to offer college membership to the growing numbers of graduate students, researchers, and lecturers in university posts without college affiliation. The intention to set up the college in Iffley was abandoned when a larger and more attractive site became available on the west bank of the Cherwell; and the name of the foundation was changed when the Wolfson Foundation offered a large grant for building, accompanied by a substantial endowment conferred by the Ford Foundation. The new, modern, buildings on the Cherwell site were completed in 1974 and the college is now one of Oxford's largest.

The outer face of Tree Quad.

WORCESTER COLLEGE

The Library.

The college occupies the site and a few of the buildings of the medieval Gloucester College set up in 1283 by the Benedictines for their scholars from Gloucester and other abbeys in the south of England. Each abbey built a cottage or camera for its scholars, and at one time fifteen abbeys were thus represented. Six of these camerae survive in the south range of the college's single quadrangle. Gloucester College was dissolved along with the monasteries in 1539, and in 1560 the buildings were acquired by Sir Thomas White who had recently founded St John's. He set up Gloucester Hall, which continued precariously as a subsidiary of St John's until in 1714 it was bought, substantially endowed and renamed, by Sir Thomas Cookes, a rich Worcestershire baronet. Dr George Clarke of All Souls, the amateur architect and a benefactor of Worcester College, had a hand in the designs for the principal neo-classical buildings, with some help from the celebrated Nicholas Hawksmoor.

The Provost's Lodgings.

The Sainsbury Building (1984).

The Lake.

Radcliffe Camera and St Mary's Church over the Thames.

BLACKWELL'S

Blackwell's, the renowned book business, is as much a feature of Oxford as are the university institutions; it was founded in 1879 by Benjamin Blackwell, who lived above the shop at 50 Broad Street; it has remained a private family company managed successively by the founder's son, his grandsons, and no doubt his great-grandsons. The firm's continuing growth has resulted in the occupation of several other buildings in The Broad and also includes the impressive Norrington Room underground below part of Trinity College; this vast room is said to contain three miles of shelving and to be the world's largest book display. Similarly, on a smaller scale, Blackwell's Music Shop in Holywell has a basement below part of Wadham College. The firm's visible business is exceeded by its mail order trade, conducted from Beaver House in Hythe Bridge Street; Blackwell's also has over 50 academic and general bookstores in the United Kingdom and is continually expanding.

ACADEMIC DRESS

The Chancellor.

Graduate Robes.

Graduate Robes.

Proctors.   The Marshal.

Graduate Robes.

Graduate Robes.

In the Middle Ages all clerks in the University – Doctors, Masters, and scholars – were obliged to wear the black *cappa*, a tent-like gown with a hood to cover the head. Over the years colours were adopted to distinguish Doctors and Masters of the different schools, and caps and bonnets of various shapes were evolved for ceremonial occasions. Today there is an elaborate code of conventions that includes a magnificent gown for the Chancellor, at least twenty-five basic colour-schemes for the various academic degrees, and special robes for the Proctors, the Marshal, the Verger, and the Bedels. All this is backed up in detailed rulings on how, when, and where, specific gowns, hoods, caps, and bonnets are to be worn, and what alternative options are permissible. Occasions such as degree-givings and *Encaenia* are when this finery is displayed.

THE OXFORD CANAL

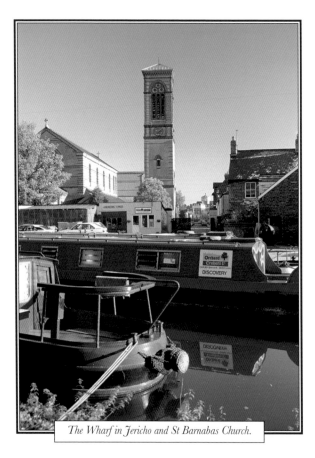

The Wharf in Jericho and St Barnabas Church.

The southern section of the Oxford Canal was opened in 1790; it connected Oxford with Coventry and with the whole English canal system. In Oxford it terminated in a large basin with wharves and coal-yards for the narrow-boats from the Midlands, and there were intermediate wharves in Jericho and at Hayfield Road. The canal had only a brief commercial life; in the second half of the 19th century it progressively lost its traffic to the railways, and by 1920 commercial movement had virtually ceased. The terminal basin was sold to Lord Nuffield in 1937 as a site for his projected college, and the canal was cut short at Hythe Bridge Street. Fortunately the general interest in canals as amenities came in time for the Oxford Canal to survive, and today it is one of England's most attractive cruising stretches; moreover it is connected with both the canal system and the Thames.

Isis Lock.

SPORT

The Thames by Christ Church Meadow.

All the classical sports and games are practised at Oxford, the colleges competing among themselves and the University with other universities, especially Cambridge. The sport that takes place in the most attractive surroundings and attracts the widest attention is undoubtedly rowing, especially the inter-college bumping races "Torpids" and "Summer Eights", and most especially the Oxford and Cambridge Boat Race. Eights Week in Oxford is a great social occasion, if not exactly as described by Max Beerbohm in Zuleika Dobson, and rowing successes are rewarded with festivities such as Bump Suppers. The rivers – Thames and Cherwell – also provide a romantic setting for the most leisurely of all diversions: punting, propelling a comfortable flat-bottomed boat with a long pole, best practised with congenial company and ample refreshments. Other activities include all the classical out-door sports, and social occasions such as the balls held in May and June at the end of the academic year.

In the University Parks.

Cricket in Worcester College grounds.

At a College Ball.

The Examination Schools.

Magdalen College School and the Cherwell.

ACKNOWLEDGEMENTS

Grateful thanks to the Colleges and the University for encouragement and
permission to reproduce the pictures, to Mr John Venables for permission to
reproduce from his book *Academic Dress of the University of Oxford*, and to the
Vice-Chancellor Sir Peter North for kindly contributing the introduction.